GROW
PALM
TREES

IN HAWAI'I AND OTHER TROPICAL CLIMATES

Library of Congress Cataloging-in-Publication Data

Leaser, David.
    Growing palms in Hawaii / David Leaser.
        p. cm.
    Includes bibliographical references and index.
    ISBN 1-56647-825-1 (softcover : alk. paper)
    1. Palms--Hawaii. I. Title.
    SB413.P17L43 2007
    635.9'774509969--dc22
                            2006101235

ISBN-13: 978-1-56647-825-0
ISBN-10: 1-56647-825-1

Image on page 13 © iStockphoto.com
Image on page 32 © Tobias Spanner
Image on page 85 © Dean Piercy
All other images © David Leaser

Front Cover: Coconut palms line the black sands of Punulu'u Beach on the Big Island of Hawai'i.

Page 1: An African oil palm graces the National Tropical Botanical Garden on Kaua'i.

This page: Betel nut palms, sealing wax palms, and a variety of other species are displayed at Ho'omaluhia Botanical Garden in Kāne'ohe on O'ahu, Hawai'i.

First Printing, June 2007
1 2 3 4 5 6 7 8 9

Mutual Publishing, LLC
1215 Center Street, Suite 210
Honolulu, Hawai'i 96816
Ph: 808-732-1709 / Fax: 808-734-4094
Email: info@mutualpublishing.com
www.mutualpublishing.com

Printed in Korea

GROWING
PALM
TREES

IN HAWAI'I AND OTHER TROPICAL CLIMATES

David Leaser

MUTUAL PUBLISHING

GROWING
PALM TREES
IN HAWAI'I AND OTHER TROPICAL CLIMATES

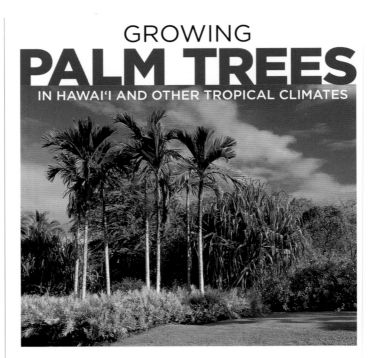

**Betel nut palms
(*Areca catechu*) add a
touch of elegance to
the Alii Marketplace
in Kailua-Kona on
the Big Island of
Hawai'i.**

Contents

Note: *The palms featured in this book will grow well in any region with a tropical climate. Similarly, the information on palm care is applicable in any location with growing conditions similar to Hawai'i.*

Native to the Carribean, thatch palms (*Thrinax radiata* and *Coccothrinax barbadensis*) grow beautifully on the Windward coast of O'ahu at Ho'omaluhia Botanical Garden in Kāne'ohe.

The Symbols of the Tropics

A BRIEF HISTORY OF PALMS IN HAWAI'I

Hawai'i is famous for its weather, its people and its spectacular beaches and sunsets. But imagine a Hawaiian sunset without the swaying fronds of a coconut palm. Indeed, the coconut palm completes the picture of paradise. Symbols of the tropics, Hawai'i's beautiful palm trees are depicted in nearly every Hawaiian postcard and travel brochure. Like the date palms that line the streets of Beverly Hills, the palms that dot the hillsides of Hawai'i are a vital part of the Hawaiian experience.

ABOVE: Part of the Honolulu Botanical Gardens system, Ho'omaluhia Botanical Garden in Kāne'ohe on O'ahu features an outstanding collection of tropical palms that can be grown in Hawai'i.

RIGHT: A small grove of coconut palms grow on an island in front of the Hawaii Tropical Botanical Garden outside Hilo on the Big Island.

Surprisingly, Hawai'i is home to only one native palm genus, *Pritchardia*, which consists of more than 20 species. Early Polynesians introduced nonnative coconut palms (*Cocos nucifera*) hundreds of years ago. Here, coconut palms tower over *Pritchardia* palms, also called loulu palms.

TOP: Coconut palms complement the view of Diamond Head from Ala Moana Park on Oʻahu.

ABOVE: Alexandra palms (*Archontophoenix alexandrae*) from Australia have naturalized in the valleys near Hilo on the Big Island of Hawaiʻi.

But palms have not always been a prominent part of the Hawaiian landscape. When the early Polynesians set foot on Hawaiʻi, the Islands were nearly devoid of palms. The first human settlers did not land on palm-fringed beaches. Only one genus, *Pritchardia*, inhabited the Islands at first contact. The coconut palm was brought by the early Polynesians to help them colonize the islands.

Like all of the "boat plants" that were introduced by the early settlers, the coconut palm's role was purely functional and utilitarian. Fronds were used for roofing, trunks were felled for timber, and coconuts were used for food and animal fodder. Nearly every part of the palm served an important role in the daily lives of early Hawaiians.

Palms add elegance to a fantasy pool at the Maui Marriott hotel at Kāʻanapali. Here coconut palms *(Cocos nucifera)* dwarf smaller pygmy date palms *(Phoenix roebelenii)* and alexandra palms *(Archontophoenix alexandrae).*

Although there are about 2,500 documented palm species, Hawai'i's palm varieties probably only consisted of two genera until the nineteeth century. The native *Pritchardia*, or loulu palm, and the introduced *Cocos nucifera*, or coconut palm, were the only palms on the Islands during the reign of Kamehameha I.

In the mid-nineteenth century, wealthy plantation owners began to introduce new and exotic varieties of palms to the Islands. Early botanists, like Dr. William Hillebrand, dramatically changed the landscape of the Islands with new species. Foster Botanical Garden, the oldest of the Honolulu Botanical Gardens, contains trees that Hillebrand planted in the 1850s.

Many of these early introductions and their offspring can still be seen on the Islands at botanical gardens, hotels, and other public and private sites. Iolani Palace is surrounded by towering old royal palms (*Roystonea regia*), introduced from Cuba, and date palms from around the world.

ABOVE: The entrance to 'Iolani Palace in Honolulu is lined with Cuban royal palms (*Roystonea regia*). Native to Cuba and Florida, these palms make ideal avenue plantings.

OPPOSITE: Loulu palms (*Pritchardia* species) accent an ancient man-made saltwater pond in the Kona district of the Big Island of Hawai'i.

By seeking out the rare and unusual, botanists and palm enthusiasts have created the diverse paradise we enjoy every day. Hawai'i is now a treasure-trove of palms from around the world, adding to the natural beauty of the Hawaiian islands. Today, with hundreds of palms to choose from and a growing number of local growers, the possibilities are almost limitless.

Distinguishing One Palm from Another

UNDERSTANDING THE STRUCTURE OF PALMS

From diminutive rain forest plants to towering trees, the selection of palms you can plant in your garden is almost unlimited. In fact, palms can be used in nearly every landscaping capacity. Smaller species can serve as ground covers, shrubby types make excellent foundation plantings, and tall, single-trunked palms can frame a view.

Palms are usually described and characterized by their trunk types and frond shapes. The following page shows the basics to help you identify them.

ABOVE: Palms make excellent landscape plants. Whether you want to frame a view or hide an eyesore, the variety of palms you can grow will astound you. With their wide range of colors, sizes, and shapes, palms are a staple for a tropical garden.

LEAVES. Also called fronds. Palmate fronds are shaped like the palm of your hand. Palms with palmate fronds are called fan palms. Pinnate fronds, shown here, are shaped like bird feathers. Palms with pinnate fronds are sometimes called feather palms.

Some palms have pinnate fronds that look plumose, like the foxtail palm (*Wodyetia bifurcata*). Others have deeply divided bipinnate leaf segments, including the fishtail palms (*Caryota* species).

SPEAR. The newest emerging frond.

CROWNSHAFT. Some palms bear a crownshaft, a tightly packed set of leaf bases just below the fronds. Crownshafts are typically green but can be any color. Palms with crownshafts are considered "self-cleaning" because their dead fronds drop cleanly from the trunk.

TRUNK. Some palms have solitary trunks, like coconut palms. Others form clumps, including lady palms (*Rhapis* species) and many *Areca* palms.

A Sampler of Landscape Palms

A SELECTION OF PALMS THAT GROW WELL IN HAWAI'I AND OTHER TROPICAL LOCALES

With about 2,500 species in 192 genera, the palm kingdom is among the most diverse in the world.

And Hawai'i is one of the best places in the world to grow palms. With its diverse climate zones, from tropical to desert, the selection of palms that grow here is indeed vast.

While there are hundreds of palms that will grow in Hawai'i, this section includes a sampler of several dozen species that are readily available through your local garden center or an online retailer, many of whom reside on the Big Island. When you visit Hawai'i's botanical gardens, chances are you will see nearly every species depicted here.

The palms in this section are listed by scientific name. The most widely used common names are also listed. Use this guide as a starting point to help you determine the best palm for your garden. You may find the cultural requirements differ in your garden because of your microclimate, soil, or gardening practices. Although palms are technically not trees, the terms *tree, plant,* and *palm* are used interchangeably in this section. Check the glossary at the end of this book to familiarize yourself with the terms commonly used to describe the various parts of the palm.

ACOELORRHAPHE WRIGHTII

Paurotis palm, Everglades palm. Native to Florida and the Caribbean, this palm grows slowly to about 40 ft./12 m. with multiple 4 in./10 cm. trunks covered with a red fiber. Fan-shaped leaves and a silvery sheen. Will grow in poor, rocky soils but should be kept well-watered and fertilized. Because of its clumping nature, this palm makes a good large screen or hedge. Prefers full sun.

ADONIDIA MERRILLII

Christmas palm, Manila palm. Native to the Philippines, this palm grows relatively quickly to more than 20 ft./6 m. tall. With its green crownshaft, pinnate fronds and red fruit, this single-trunked palm makes a great specimen for small gardens or containers in sunny interiors. Often seen planted in groupings of three or more plants. Grows in full sun to part shade and needs ample water.

ARCHONTOPHOENIX ALEXANDRAE

Alexandra palm. Native to Australia, this single-trunked palm grows to more than 40 ft./12 m. tall. Bearing a green crownshaft, a gray trunk and pinnate fronds, this palm prefers moist soils but is not tolerant of salt. Bears white flowers followed by red fruit. A good palm for avenues or as a grouping, the Alexandra palm has naturalized in Hawai'i, particularly in the North Hilo district.

ARCHONTOPHOENIX CUNNINGHAMIANA

King palm. Native to Australia, this palm is similar to *A. alexandrae*, but bears attractive lavender flowers. A single-trunked palm with a green crownshaft topped by pinnate fronds, this tree grows relatively quickly to more than 60 ft./18 m. tall. Not fussy about soils, but prefers adequate moisture. Often seen in nurseries as a grouping of three or more plants. Looks good in sun or shade.

ARECA IPOT

Highland betel nut palm. Native to the Philippines, this palm is a good small-scale alternative to *A. catechu*. Grows to 15 ft./5 m. tall and sports a beautiful green crownshaft and large colorful fruit. An excellent palm that will thrive in full shade with ample water. Fruit is also used as a mild narcotic in some cultures.

ARECA VESTIARIA

Orange collar palm. From tropical Southeast Asia, this palm makes a colorful addition to the landcape. Its crownshafts range from orange to red and fruit is bright red. The new pinnate leaves of some species are reddish maroon. Grows to more than 20 ft./6 m. tall as a large clump. Needs ample water and partial shade to look its best. This is a perfect palm for an accent, entranceway or lanai.

ARENGA ENGLERI

Dwarf sugar palm, Formosa palm. Native to Taiwan and the Ryuku Islands, this clumping palm with pinnate fronds grows to about 15 ft./5 m. tall with an equal spread. Makes a great screen or accent for sunny areas. Needs a moderate amount of water. The yellow flowers of this palm are fragrant and are followed by fruit with stinging crystals of calcium oxalate which irritate the skin.

BACTRIS GASIPAES

Peach palm. Ranging from Central to South America, this clumping palm with pinnate fronds grows to more than 25 ft./7 m. tall. Thrives in full sun to part shade with regular water and fertilizer. The large yellow-orange fruit (as is the heart of the palm) is edible and is used as a food source in its native countries.

BENTINCKIA NICOBARICA

Nicobar palm. Native to the Nicobar Islands in the Bay of Bengal, this single-trunked palm with pinnate fronds grows to more than 50 ft./15 m. tall. Trunks are deep gray and have attractive whitish rings, topped by a grayish-green crownshaft. Grows well in full sun to shade in moist soils. A dramatic, attractive palm which looks good when planted in groups.

BISMARCKIA NOBILIS

Bismarck palm. Native to Madagascar, this single-trunked palm is topped by massive grayish blue palmate fronds. Grows to more than 30 ft./9 m. tall, more than twice that in its native habitat. Prefers full sun and moderate water, but is not tolerant of sea spray. Frond color is highly variable from green to a silvery-gray color. A perfect accent for a large garden or yard.

BRAHEA ARMATA

Mexican blue fan palm, blue hesper palm. Native to Baja California, Mexico. This single-trunked palm with palmate fronds grows slowly to 40 ft./12 m. tall. Bears attractive blue-gray fronds and a "petticoat" made of dead fronds, shown trimmed here. Grows best in full sun and is highly drought tolerant, making it a good palm for Leeward gardens. This palm will grow in dry rocky areas.

BUTIA CAPITATA

Pindo palm, jelly palm. Native to South America, this single-trunked palm with pinnate fronds grows to about 20 ft./6 m. tall, making it a great palm for smaller gardens. Fronds range in color from green to silvery gray. This palm grows well in full sun with moderate water, making it a good choice for gardens with lower rainfall. Attractive yellow to red fruit is edible and used to make jelly.

CALYPTROCALYX HOLLRUNGII

Hollrung's palm. Native to New Guinea, this clumping palm with undivided pinnate fronds grows to about 8 ft./2 m. tall. With its thin stems and small crownshafts, this palm makes an ideal plant for small gardens. Also makes a great container plant. New emerging fronds are reddish brown to maroon. Grows well in partial shade with ample water.

CARPENTARIA ACUMINATA

Carpentaria palm. Native to Australia, this single-trunked palm grows relatively quickly to at least 30 ft./9 m. tall, often much taller. Trunk is gray with prominent rings and is topped by a crown of pinnate fronds. Prefers full sun and moist soil. Not fussy about soil type, but does not tolerate seaside conditions.

CARYOTA MITIS

Clustering fishtail palm. Native to India and Southeast Asia, this clumping palm grows to more than 15 ft./5 m., sometimes double that size. Multiple thin stems are covered with fishtail-shaped leaflets in a light green color. Makes a great hedge or screen and is suitable for sunny lanais and indoor containers. Prefers full sun and ample water. Not tolerant of salty soils.

CARYOTA OBTUSA

Black fishtail palm. Native to Thailand and India, this single-trunked tree bears a massive crown of bipinnate fronds with fishtail-shaped leaflets. A fast growing tree to 60 ft./18 m., this palm makes an impressive statement in a large garden. Upon maturity, usually after 20 or more years, this palm will flower and die. Needs ample water and grows in partial shade to full sun.

CARYOTA URENS

Wine palm, toddy palm, jaggery palm. Native to Burma, India, and Malaysia, this single-trunked palm grows to more than 50 ft./15 m. tall. With its stout gray trunk and fishtail-shaped leaflets, this palm makes a great accent to a large garden. Fast growing, this tree makes a good windscreen. Prefers full sun and ample water. Like *C. obtusa*, this palm will die upon maturity.

CHAMAEDOREA METALLICA

Metallic palm, miniature fishtail palm. Native to Mexico, this single-trunked palm grows to more than 5 ft./2 m. tall. Leaves are undivided and have a silvery sheen. This palm looks best when planted in groupings of three or more plants. Prefers full shade and ample water. Makes a good accent for a courtyard or lanai. Excellent container specimen.

CHAMAEDOREA MICROSPADIX

Hardy bamboo palm. Native to Mexico, this clumping palm grows to about 10 ft./3 m. tall and makes a good palm for shady gardens. Pinnate fronds are dull green. Bright red fruit provides an attractive accent. Good as a hedge, screen, or container specimen. Stems bear a resemblance to bamboo.

CHAMAEDOREA SEIFRIZII

Bamboo palm, reed palm. Native to Mexico and Central America, this small clumping palm grows to 10 ft./3 m. tall and bears dull green pinnate fronds and bamboo-like stems. An ideal palm for shady entrance areas or as a small-scale screen, this palm prefers shade and ample water. Makes a great container or in-door specimen. Left unthinned, this palm will form leaves from the ground up.

CHAMAEROPS HUMILIS

European fan palm, Mediterranean fan palm. Native to Europe and Africa, this clumping palm with palmate fronds grows slowly to 20 ft./6 m. tall. This palm makes an attractive accent for the sunny, arid garden. Highly tolerant of dry, rocky soils and strong winds. Many forms exist, with leaf colors ranging from green to silver gray. Fronds bear sharp spines.

CHAMBEYRONIA MACROCARPA

Flamethrower. Native to New Caledonia, this single-trunked palm is highly ornamental. New fronds open in shades of scarlet, orange, or maroon, fading to green. The crownshaft color is also variable, from deep green to pale ivory. This palm grows slowly to more than 20 ft./6 m. tall, sometimes double that size in ideal growing conditions. Needs ample water and prefers full sun to part shade.

CLINOSTIGMA SAMOENSE

Samoan palm. Native to Samoa, this single-trunked palm with pinnate fronds grows to 60 ft./18 m. tall. This palm is highly ornamental, sporting a prominent green crownshaft and finely divided fronds. Requires copious amounts of water.

COCCOTHRINAX ARGENTATA

Florida silver palm. Native to Florida, Mexico, and the Caribbean, this small single-trunked palm bears attractive palmate fronds. Grows slowly to 15 ft./5 m. in full sun. These small-scale palms look great when planted in groupings or used as a foundation planting. Tolerant of poor soil, coastal conditions, and drought, but look best with moderate water.

COCCOTHRINAX CRINATA

Old man thatch palm. Native to Cuba, this single-trunked palm with palmate fronds grows to about 8 ft./2 m. tall and is covered with a thick, wool-like fiber. Will tolerate partial shade, but looks best when planted in full sun. Needs moderate water, but will tolerate harsh conditions, including rocky soils and coastal areas. Good drainage is a necessity. An interesting novelty in the garden.

COCOS NUCIFERA

Coconut palm, niu. Named for the Portuguese word for monkey, the coconut palm is of unknown origin. Early Polynesians brought coconuts to Hawai'i hundreds of years ago, and they have naturalized along most coastal areas. All are single-trunked palms with pinnate fronds and edible fruit. Highly variable, ranging from dwarf forms to trees that grow to more than 100 ft./30 m. tall.

COPERNICIA PRUNIFERA

Carnauba wax palm. Native to Brazil, this single-trunked palm with palmate fronds grows slowly to 35 ft./11 m. Leaves are bluish gray, covered with wax that is harvested to make car and floor wax. Prefers full sun and moderate watering, making it a great palm for dry, windy areas. Needs good drainage. Several species of *Copernicia* grow well in Hawai'i, and all are very slow growers.

CORYPHA UTAN

Talipot palm. Native to India, Australia, and Southeast Asia. This single-trunked palm bears massive palmate fronds that are nearly 20 ft./6 m. wide. Growing to more than 70 ft./21 m. tall, this palm bears the largest flower stalk in the plant kingdom, after which the palm declines and dies. Makes a great statement in a large garden. Needs full sun and ample water.

CYRTOSTACHYS RENDA

Sealing wax palm. Native to Borneo, Thailand, and Malaysia, this is one of the most striking palms. A clumping palm with pinnate fronds, this palm bears stunning bright red crownshafts, the color of colonial British letter sealing wax. Looks especially attractive as a younger specimen. Grows to 35 ft./11 m. tall in sun to partial shade. Needs ample water and can be grown in boggy areas.

DECKENIA NOBILIS

Noble palm. Native to the rain forests of the Seychelle Islands, this single-trunked palm with pinnate fronds grows to 100 ft./33 m. or more. Trunk is a light tan or gray with distinctive dark rings. Bears a light green to purplish crownshaft. This is a beautiful palm for gardens with full sun, rich soil, and ample water. Trunk is covered with spines when young, limiting use near walkways.

DYPSIS DECARYI

Triangle palm. Native to Madagascar, this single-trunked palm can grow to 30 ft./9 m. tall. Gray-green pinnate fronds grow in groups of three, giving the trunk's apex a triangular look. Grows and looks best in full sun with a moderate amount of water. Can also tolerate arid conditions, making it a good palm for Leeward gardens with low rainfall.

DYPSIS LUTESCENS

Areca palm, butterfly palm. Native to Madagascar, this palm forms a massive clump of yellowish trunks and pale green pinnate fronds. Grows to about 20 ft./6 m. tall with an equal spread. Makes a great large-scale screen or accent. Excellent container or indoor palm. Thin out some of the trunks to accent the attractive ringed trunks. Prefers ample water and sun to partial shade.

ELAEIS GUINEENSIS

African oil palm. Native to Africa, this single-trunked palm grows to more than 35 ft./11 m. tall. Topped by a full crown of large, drooping fronds, this massive palm requires a large area. Makes a great avenue planting. One of the most important palms economically, its fruit and seeds are pressed to create oil used for a variety of purposes. Spiny petioles limit use near walkways and pools.

EUTERPE EDULIS

Cabbage palm. Native to Brazil, this palm grows to about 20 ft./6 m. tall. With its small size and and arching pinnate fronds, this palm makes a perfect addition to the small garden. Its gray-brown trunk is topped by a prominent green crown-shaft. Makes a great container specimen and indoor plant. In South America, these palms are grown on large plantations and harvested for hearts of palm.

HEDYSCEPE CANTERBURYANA

Umbrella palm, big mountain palm. Native to Lord Howe Island in the South Pacific, this single-trunked palm sports a bulging silvery green crownshaft and a crown of stiff green, pinnate fronds. Growing to 35 ft./11 m. tall, this palm makes a great specimen in the garden or as a container plant when young. Prefers partial shade to full sun and needs well-drained soil. Needs moderate water.

HETEROSPATHE ELATA

Sagisi palm. Native to the Philippines, this single-trunked palm grows to 40 ft./12 m. tall. An elegant palm with graceful pinnate fronds which are pinkish when first emerging. This tree has become an invasive species on Guam, so take care when planting near rural areas. Prefers partial shade, especially when young. Needs ample water.

HOWEA FORSTERIANA

Kentia palm, parlor palm. Native to Lord Howe Island, this single-trunked palm with pinnate fronds grows to 40 ft./12 m. tall. Long grown as as greenhouse plant, starting in Victorian England, this palm is an ideal houseplant for areas with strong indirect light. Grows well in full sun to shade and needs a moderate amount of water. Excellent palm for coastal areas.

HYOPHORBE INDICA

Champagne bottle palm. Native to the Mascarene Islands in the Indian Ocean, this single-trunked palm grows quickly to 20 ft./6 m. tall, making it an ideal palm for the small garden. This palm's gray trunk is topped by a deep green crownshaft and a sparse crown of arching pinnate fronds. Young seedlings are variable in color; some have red stems that fade to green as they mature.

HYOPHORBE LAGENICAULIS

Bottle palm. Native to the Mascarene Islands in the Indian Ocean, this palm has an unusual bulging trunk, giving it a bottle-like appearance. Attractive green crownshaft is topped by a sparse crown of stiff fronds. This is an excellent novelty plant and makes a great container specimen for poolside areas, patios, and lanais. Grows to 10 ft./3 m. tall. Prefers sun to partial shade with ample water.

HYOPHORBE VERSCHAFFELTII

Spindle palm. Native to the Mascarene Islands in the Indian Ocean. This single-trunked palm with a sparse crown of pinnate fronds grows to 15 ft./5 m. tall. With its swollen gray trunk and attractive blue-green crownshaft, this tree makes a beautiful accent in the garden. Especially attractive when planted in groups of three or more. This palm need ample water and full sun.

JOHANNESTEIJSMANNIA ALTIFRONS

Joey palm, diamond joey. Native to Southeast Asia, this trunkless palm bears wedge-shaped fronds that can reach more than 20 ft./6 m. in length. Requires copious amounts of water and protection from the elements to look its best. Wind and snails will destroy its fronds. Grows best in full shade.

KENTIOPSIS OLIVIFORMIS

Native to New Caledonia, this single-trunked palm grows to 90 ft./27 m. and bears a prominently ringed trunk that is greenish-gray. Its prominent pale green crownshaft is topped by stiff pinnate fronds. Prefers partial shade to full sun and needs a moderate amount of water.

LACCOSPADIX AUSTRALASICA

Atherton palm. Native to Australia, this palm looks like a small-scale kentia palm. Grows to at least 12 ft./4 m. tall. Sometimes seen as a clumping palm or a single-trunked specimen. Trunk is gray with distinctive rings and topped by a thick crown of pinnate fronds, sometimes emerging in shades of reddish maroon. Attractive red fruit adds seasonal appeal. Prefers partial shade and ample water.

LATANIA LODDIGESII

Blue latan palm. Native to the Mascarene Islands, this single-trunked palm grows to 30 ft./9 m. or more and has striking gray palmate fronds. Bears a passing resemblance to *Bismarckia nobilis*, but leaves are less stiff and the trunk flares at the base. Prefers full sun to partial shade and a moderate amount of water. Tolerant of drought and poor rocky soils.

LICUALA GRANDIS

Licuala palm. Native to the Solomon Islands and Vanuatu, this single-trunked tree grows to about 10 ft./3 m. tall, making it a great palm for small gardens or courtyards. Attracive palmate fronds are undivided and nearly circular. Grows in shade to partial sun and needs ample water. This is a good palm for containers or small spaces provided you protect from heavy winds.

LICUALA PELTATA

Elegant palm. Native to Malaysia, India, Bangladesh, and Thailand, this is another beautiful plant for shady gardens. This single-trunked palm grows to about 20 ft./6 m. tall and is topped by a full crown of nearly orbital fronds. Some forms have divided leaves, others are nearly whole. Likes shade and ample water.

LICUALA RAMSAYI

Native to Australia, this single-trunked palm can reach 60 ft./18 m. tall, but is usually seen as a younger tree of less than half that height. Wedge-shaped leaves are deeply divided. Bears attractive orange fruit. A good palm for shady areas with ample moisture. Also makes a good container specimen for a shady patio or courtyard.

LIVISTONA AUSTRALIS

Australian fan palm. Native to Australia, this single-trunked palm grows to 50 ft./15 m. tall and is topped by a crown of palmate fronds. Looks similar to *Washingtonia robusta,* but is more elegant and fronds are much shinier. Excellent avenue planting which can serve as a container plant when young. Needs full sun and a moderate amount of water. Spiny petioles limit usage near play areas.

LIVISTONA CHINENSIS

Chinese fan palm. Native to Taiwan and Japan, this palm is similar to *L. austra-lis,* but does not grow as tall, making it an ideal alternative for smaller gardens. A single-trunked plant with shiny, droopy, palmate fronds, this palm grows to 20 ft./6 m. tall and prefers full sun. A great plant for containers on patios and lanais. Fairly salt and drought tolerant.

LODOICEA MALDIVICA

Double coconut. Native to the Seychelle Islands, this attractive fan palm grows to 80 ft./24 m. tall from a large seed, the largest in the plant world. Slow growing, sometimes taking a decade to form a trunk, this palm is a great novelty plant. Rarely seen outside botanical gardens (you can see several at Foster Botanical Garden and Limahuli Gardens), seeds are now readily available, but expensive.

LYTOCARYUM WEDDELLIANUM

Victorian parlor palm. Native to southeastern Brazil, this single-trunked palm grows to 12 ft./4 m. tall. With its shiny dark green pinnate fronds, this palm makes a great addition to the shady garden. Grows best in partial shade with ample water. This plant makes a great container specimen and grows well indoors.

METROXYLON WARBURGII

Sagu palm. Native to Vanuatu and western Samoa. This single-trunked palm grows quickly to at least 23 ft./7 m. tall and bears a crown of stiff upright fronds. Several species in this genus can be spotted throughout the Islands' botanical gardens. All require ample water and partial shade to full sun. All palms in this genus, except for *M. amicarum*, die after flowering.

NEOVEITCHIA STORCKII

Unleito palm. Native to Fiji, this single-trunked palm grows to 40 ft./12 m. tall and bears a full crown of pinnate fronds. The crownshaft on this trunk is an attractive chocolate brown to black in color. Needs full sun and ample water to look its best. In Fiji, these palms are felled and used for lumber.

NORMANBYA NORMANBYI

Black palm. Native to Australia, this palm rarely grows to more than 15 ft./5 m. in cultivation, but can reach three times that height in its native habitat. This single-trunked tree bears a light green crownshaft and a full crown of plumose fronds. Makes a great container plant or specimen for small gardens. Prefers partial shade to full sun and needs ample water to look its best.

PELAGODOXA HENRYANA

Marquesas palm. Native to the Marquesas Islands, where it is nearly extinct, this single-trunked palm with large, undivided leaves is exceptionally attractive. Grows to about 25 ft./8 m. tall. Needs copious amounts of water and protection from wind to look its best. Fruit is baseball-sized and has a warty texture.

PHOENIX RECLINATA

Senegal date palm. Native to Africa, this clumping palm grows to 30 ft./9 m. tall and can spread to more than 25 ft./8 m. Trunks arch gracefully and are topped by drooping green fronds. If left unpruned, this palm makes a good large-scale screen or barrier; spines on the petioles near the fronds make this palm a living fence. Prefers full sun and is wind and drought tolerant.

PHOENIX ROEBELENII

Pygmy date palm. Native to Laos, this is an excellent palm for containers and small gardens. Growing slowly to 20 ft./6 m. tall, this single-trunked tree is topped by a crown of shiny green pinnate fronds. As a young plant, this palm is frequently confused with ferns until it forms a trunk. Can also be used for sunny interiors. Likes full sun to partial shade and ample water.

PHOENIX SYLVESTRIS

Silver date palm, wild date palm. Native to India and neighboring countries, this single-trunked palm grows to 40 ft./12 m. tall and bears a full crown of blue-green pinnate fronds. In India, the sap from the flower stalk is used to make sugar. Fruit is edible and similar to dates found in grocery stores. Hybrids of this palm have naturalized in Hawai'i. Needs full sun and moderate water.

PINANGA CORONATA

Coronata palm, ivory cane palm. Native to Java and Sumatra, this clumping palm grows to 10 ft./3 m. Stems are bamboo-like and topped by attractive yellowish ivory crownshafts and pinnate fronds. Ideal palms for use as hedges, screens, and accents. Grows well as a container palm or foundation planting in protected courtyards. Prefers partial shade to full sun and requires ample water.

PRITCHARDIA AFFINIS

Kona fan palm, loulu palm. Native to the Big Island of Hawai'i, this single-trunked palm with palmate fronds grows to about 30 ft./9 m. tall. Needs full sun to partial shade and a moderate amount of water. Leaves are bright green. This is a great palm for nearly any area of Hawai'i and tolerates seaside conditions.

PRITCHARDIA ARECINA

Loulu palm. Native to Maui, Hawai'i, this single-trunked palm grows to 40 ft./12 m. tall. Visitors to Maui can see native stands on the Hāna coast and several grow in front of Pi'ilanihale Heiau at Kahanu Gardens. Like other loulu palms, prefers moderate water and well-drained soil.

PRITCHARDIA HILLEBRANDII 'BLUE FORM'

Blue loulu palm. Native to Moloka'i, this form of the common green loulu palm bears stunning blue-gray fronds. An oddity for Hawai'i, as most palms with blue-gray fronds come from sunny, arid areas. The blue color is actually a protective waxy coating on a green leaf. This palm deserves a special place in nearly any setting on the Islands. Grows to 25 ft./8 m. in full sun. Moderate water.

PRITCHARDIA LOWREYANA

Loulu palm. Native to Moloka'i. Another great endemic palm, this species grows to only 12 ft./4 m. tall, making it a perfect accent for small, native Hawaiian gardens. Visit Foster Botanical Garden to see a specimen, pictured here, that is more than 100 years old.

PRITCHARDIA PACIFICA

Fiji fan palm. Native to Tonga, this single-trunked palm grows to 25 ft./8 m. tall and bears a full crown of roundish green palmate fronds. Some consider this palm to be one of the most attractive in the genus.

PRITCHARDIA REMOTA

Nihoa palm. Native to the remote unihabited Hawaiian island of Nihoa, this single-trunked palm grows to 18 ft./6 m. tall. Bears a crown of bright green palmate fronds. May be more wind tolerant than most.

PRITCHARDIA THURSTONII

Thurston palm. Native to Fiji, this palm is similar to *P. pacifica*, but grows taller and produces an inflorescence that arches up and beyond the leaves. Bears a full crown of bright green palmate fronds that are slightly diamond-shaped. Moderately salt tolerant.

PTYCHOSPERMA ELEGANS

Solitaire palm. Native to Australia, this single-trunked palm with pinnate fronds grows to 20 ft./6 m. tall. Attractive, thin trunks are gray with prominent rings. Needs full sun and good drainage. Prefers ample water. Makes a good container specimen for the lanai or sunny interior.

RHAPIS EXCELSA

Lady palm. Native to Japan and China, this clumping palm creates a dense hedge-like shrub, making it ideal as a screen or foundation plant. Leaves are palmate and deeply divided. Grows to 12 ft./4 m. tall and bears multiple, thin trunks that are covered with a wooly brown fiber. Moderately drought tolerant, this palm prefers partial shade. Makes a great indoor palm.

ROYSTONEA OLERACEA

South American royal palm. Shown on the right in this photo, this palm is easily identified from other *Roystonea* species because is fronds are always upright, never drooping below a horizontal plane. Native to the Caribbean and South America, this single-trunked palm grows to 150 ft./46 m. tall. Its massive, gray trunk is topped by a bright green crownshaft.

ROYSTONEA REGIA

Cuban royal palm. Native to Cuba and Florida. Grows to 60 ft./18 m. tall, its massive trunk is topped by an emerald green crownshaft and full crown of plumose fronds. The most commonly grown species of the genus, the Cuban royal palm has naturalized in Hawai'i. Old specimens can be seen at 'Iolani Palace and many resorts. Moderately drought and salt tolerant. Good for windy areas.

SATAKENTIA LIUKIUENSIS

Satake palm. Native to the Ryuku Islands of Japan, this single-trunked palm with pinnate fronds grows to 30 ft./9 m. tall. Its slender gray trunk is topped by a purplish crownshaft and dark green fronds. Emerging leaves are sometimes purplish maroon in color. Bears a passing resemblance to the coconut palm with a greenish, ringed trunk. Grows in partial shade to full sun. Needs ample water.

SYAGRUS ROMANZOFFIANA

Queen palm. Native to Brazil, this single-trunked palm grows to 65 ft./20 m. tall. Pinnate fronds are plumose in appearance. Makes a good avenue planting and is relatively wind, salt, and drought tolerant. Prefers full sun. The *Syagrus* genus is the closest relative of the coconut and many species bear edible fruit, but not this one – its fruit are used for cattle fodder in Brazil.

THRINAX RADIATA

Florida thatch palm. Native to Florida, the Caribbean, Mexico, and Belize. This small, single-trunked palm grows to 16 ft./5 m. tall and bears palmate fronds. White fruit is highly ornamental. This palm is drought, wind and salt tolerant, making it ideal for small, coastal gardens or container planting. Will grow in nearly any well-draining soil.

VEITCHIA ARECINA

Montgomery palm. Native to Vanuatu, this single-trunked palm with pinnate fronds bears a ringed trunk and a greenish-gray crownshaft. Needing full sun and ample water to look its best, this palm will also grow well as a container specimen. Grows quickly to 30 ft./9 m. tall with a slender trunk.

VERSCHAFFELTIA SPLENDIDA

Seychelles stilt palm. Native to the Seychelles, this single-trunked palm grows to 30 ft./9 m. tall. With its undivided fronds, prominent crownshaft and stilt-like roots, this palm is highly ornamental. Trunks are covered with thin black spines, limiting its use near walkways, pools, and gardens with children. Prefers full sun and ample water.

WALLICHIA DISTICHA

Wallich palm. Native to the Himalayas, this palm grows to 30 ft./10 m. tall. Bears unusual wedge-shaped leaflets that are shiny green. Needs ample water and will grow in full sun to partial shade. After the palm bears fruit, it will turn brown and die. Fruit is covered with stinging crystals of oxalic acid which cause discomfort if handled.

WASHINGTONIA FILIFERA

California fan palm. Native to California, this single-trunked palm with palmate fronds grows to 60 ft./18 m. tall. This is the only native palm to the state of California and an ideal specimen for dry, rocky areas. Highly drought and wind tolerant and not fussy about soils. Trunk is more stout than its relative, *W. robusta*. The trunks of the palms in this photo are blackened from repeated fires.

WASHINGTONIA ROBUSTA

Mexican fan palm. Native to Mexico, this single-trunked palm grows to 100 ft./30 m. tall. Commonly seen along the streets of Los Angeles and Beverly Hills, this palm grows quickly in dry, Leeward areas of Hawai'i. Much taller and more slender than *W. filifera*, but equally drought and wind tolerant. Needs a large garden because of its size.

WODYETIA BIFURCATA

Foxtail palm. Native to Australia, this single-trunked palm with pinnate fronds grows to 30 ft./9 m. tall and looks like a miniature royal (*Roystonea*) palm. With its pale green crownshaft and dense crown of plumose fronds, this palm is ideal for smaller gardens. Makes an excellent avenue planting. Relatively drought and wind tolerant, this palm prefers moist soil and full sun.

The Right Palm for Your Garden

A CHECKLIST TO HELP YOU CHOOSE THE RIGHT PALM FOR YOUR LOCATION

Coconut palms are beautiful, but their falling nuts can be deadly. And the spines of a date palm can cause serious injury. More than one palm lover has chosen the wrong palm for their location. Here's a checklist to help you select the right palm:

Size and spread. A small one-gallon palm may grow to more than 80 ft./24 m. tall with a 20 ft./6 m. spread. Make sure you know the ultimate height of the palm you are planting. And, perhaps more important, understand the spread. A palm may only

ABOVE: Because of their salt and wind tolerance, spindle palms (*Hyophorbe verschaffeltii*) make great seaside plants. Palms that are native to shady, wet rain forests, like *Chamaedorea* species, would suffer in these conditions.

reach 20 ft./6 m. tall, but it may eventually form a large clump. The good news is that palms are very predictable in their growth; you simply need to plan for their mature size. Before you plant, take note of power lines and proximity to walkways and match your palm's ultimate size to your intended location.

Light. Make sure you know the light requirements of the palm you are planting and match its needs with your location. Also, consider future sun availability if you have planted other trees in the area. Will they eventually block the light?

Water needs. If you live in a dry area of the Islands, choose a drought-tolerant species, like *Chamaerops humilis,* or install a drip irrigation system to grow more water-thirsty species. If you are planting amongst tropicals, choose a water-loving tree, like *Cyrtostachys renda.* Many drought-tolerant palms will suffer in areas that receive too much water unless their location is carefully chosen. Plant in full sun on a slope to achieve excellent drainage.

Trunk type. Do you want to frame a view or block one? To frame a vista, choose a tall, single-trunked palm, like *Roystonea regia.* To block an unattractive view, choose a clumping palm, like *Rhapis excelsa* or *Dypsis lutescens.*

Leaf type. Really a matter of preference, palms with feathery leaves seem to evoke the tropics more than palms with fan-shaped leaves. (Interestingly, the only native palms to Hawai'i are fan palms.) Most palm gardens mix fan palms with feather palms to add visual interest.

Salinity tolerance. Typically, palms that are native to coastal areas are more salt-tolerant than palms that are native to the tropics. Palms absorb salt from soil, the water they receive, and air usually in the form of sea spray. If you live in a coastal area, pay particular attention to the salinity tolerance of the species.

Spines. Some of the most beautiful palms, like *Verschaffeltii splendida,* are armed with spines. Do you have children or pets? Or is your location near a walkway or pool? Make sure you consider the dangers of planting spiny palms.

Indoor potential. There is no such thing as an indoor palm. Palms grow outdoors, but we can simulate outdoor growing conditions by moderating temperature, humidity, light, and moisture. Some palms are surprisingly adaptable to indoor growing.

Growing Perfect Palms Perfectly

PLANTING BASICS YOU SHOULD KNOW BEFORE YOU PUT YOUR PALM IN THE GROUND

ABOVE: Tall, sun-tolerant trees provide a canopy for shade lovers. Each palm has its own unique cultural requirements that include sun exposure, water needs, and salt tolerance. By knowing your palm's special needs and choosing the right location, you can dramatically reduce the amount of time and expense needed to make your palm thrive.

Planting a palm requires you choose the right location, acclimate the palm to the new surroundings, and prepare the location for planting. A palm planted properly in the right location will be a joy for years; conversely, a palm planted in the wrong location will create headaches and additional maintenance.

Location is one of the key factors to your success. Make sure you match your location to the growing requirements of the species you are planting.

Here are a few factors you should consider:

Sun. Every species has a varying degree of sun tolerance. Some, like most rain forest palms, will thrive in shady areas or cloudy climates. Others that are native to coastal areas or deserts need full sun to survive. For example, most palms from the *Areca* and *Chamaedorea* genera will sunburn in dry coastal areas. Conversely, palms like the Bismarck palm (*Bismarckia nobilis*) look best in full sun. If you want to plant shade-loving palms in a sunny area, provide a canopy of taller trees or a man-made structure that filters out half of the light.

Wind. Dry winds can dessicate the fronds of many species. Most palms are fairly tolerant of wind, but if you live in an area that receives above-normal amounts of gusty winds, plant a species that is tolerant of dry winds. Palms like the blue hesper palm (*Brahea armata*) and the date palm (*Phoenix* species) can tolerate harsh winds and show no signs of damage. To protect sensitive species, plant near a structure or natural windbreak.

Salt. Most coastal palms can tolerate high levels of salinity in the air and soil; palms that are native to inland areas will usually show various levels of frond damage. If you live in an area with coastal breezes or saline soil, plant salt-tolerant palms like coconut palms (*Cocos nucifera*).

Soil. Good soils allow air and water to reach the roots of your palm. Without air, palms cannot uptake vital nutrients. Most palms prefer soil with a mixture of organic and inorganic materials, although some, like coconut palms, grow well in pure sand. If you live in an area with pure cinders or heavy clay, you can amend your soil with organic matter. As a rule, your soil should retain enough water to nourish the plant without allowing the roots to become waterlogged. If you live in an area with pure cinders and very little rainfall, install a drip irrigation system to allow water to slowly trickle onto the palm's roots.

Drainage. To determine drainage if you do not live in a lava area, dig a two-foot deep hole in the area you plan to plant. Fill the hole with water and wait for it to drain out. Then fill the hole with water again. If the hole empties in an hour or two, your drainage is good. If the water remains longer, your soil drains poorly, and you should try another location or create a raised planting bed.

Soil amendments. Organic matter should be fully composted before you add it to your soil. Choose an organic amendment that is clean and free of weed seeds. Well-rotted manure makes a good choice, but water thoroughly to leach out excess salt. Peat helps sandy or rocky areas retain moisture. Coir, a by-product of the coconut palm, is similar to peat. Wood chips, tree bark, and sawdust will also provide organic material, but they may leach nitrogen from the soil as they decompose. Add nitrogren fertilizer to the mix if you are using these products.

Organic matter provides an added benefit: It lowers the pH level of the soil. A pH is a measure of alkalinity and acidity. The higher the pH number, the more alkaline. Most palms prefer soil that is slightly acidic. Check the pH of your soil with an inexpensive test kit available at most garden centers. In general, palms prefer a pH level between 6 and 7. The Agricultural Diagnostic Service Center at the University of Hawai'i in Mānoa offers a low-cost soil and plant tissue testing service that includes a complete diagnosis and recommended fertilizer routine.

ACCLIMATE YOUR PALMS BEFORE YOU PLANT

Most palms are grown in shadehouses or greenhouses and are accustomed to low light levels and high levels of humidity. Any changes to the environment will temporarily shock your palm. Palms often "sulk" after they are planted, sometimes for a year or more. Until they acclimate, many palms will cease growth and decline slightly, exhibiting signs of stress.

Size and age will affect your palm's ability to acclimate. Young seedlings may succumb to inclement conditions, while mature trees suffer minor setbacks. Before you plant permanently in the ground, make sure your palm has a fully developed root system.

If you are planting a palm that has grown in a shadehouse, you may need to gradually expose the plant to its new environment to prevent the fronds from burning. If you are planting in a garden that receives full sun, you may want to keep the palm in its container and gradually increase the amount of sun it receives, lengthening the duration every few days until the palm is fully acclimated to the sun.

PLANTING STEP-BY-STEP

❶ Dig a hole that is the exact depth of the container and twice as wide as the opening. Never plant too deeply; trees planted too deeply may suffocate or rot. Conversely, trees planted too shallow form weak roots that dry out and burn.

❷ Place palm fertilizer in the hole before you plant. Adding fertilizer to the hole (rather than the surface) will prevent excess weeds from growing around the newly planted tree. Use caution: Fertilizers can burn sensitive roots, so spread a layer of soil over the fertilizer and follow the manufacturer's recommendations.

❸ Place the palm in the center of the hole. Make sure the base of the palm's trunk is level with the surrounding ground. Use a stick or the handle of a shovel to check. If the hole is too deep, add soil under the palm and tamp down firmly to remove any air pockets. Fill in around the root ball with soil.

❹ Spread a cup of Epsom salts on the soil. Epsom salts are a granular form of magnesium, important in the root production of palms. A cup per palm contains enough magnesium to help your tree establish roots in its new environment.

❺ Water deeply. A thorough watering will settle the soil and remove excess air pockets. Water the palm again in a few days. New and disturbed soils sometimes repel water, so check on the palm between waterings. Keep the soil moist, not soggy, for the first four months.

Digging and Moving Palms

MOST PALMS CAN BE TRANSPLANTED EASILY IF YOU FOLLOW THESE STEPS

Most mature palms are easy to transplant. Unlike many other trees, you can transplant a sizeable tree with a relatively small root ball. Here are a few pointers:

Root regeneration. Unlike many trees, palms regenerate new roots to replace those that have been cut. Typically, a large percentage of the severed roots wither away and are replaced by new roots. Some genera, including *Sabal*, rely entirely on newly regenerated roots, so it is unnecessary to dig and transplant a large root ball. Depend-

ABOVE: Palms can be transplanted with surprisingly small root balls; some species, like these *Sabal* palms, will completely regenerate new roots from the base of the trunk. If you are not replanting immediately, make sure you protect the roots by wrapping them with burlap or plastic and keep the remaining soil moist.

ing on the species, severed root stubs will branch and form new roots or drop off completely. Within months, the tree will regenerate roots directly from the trunk. Many palms, like Bismarck palms (*Bismarckia nobilis*) benefit from root pruning. About 60 days before transplanting, dig a sharp spade into the ground about 12 in./30 cm. away from the trunk. The palm will begin regenerating new roots which can uptake water after final digging.

Digging the root ball. Wet the area around the base of the palm to help the soil cling to the roots. Dig a root ball about 12-18 in./30-46 cm. from the base of the trunk. Dig down about 24-30 in./61-76 cm. to retain as much depth as possible. Use a shovel to measure the distance or mark the ground with spray paint to determine the root ball size.

Moving the palm. If the soil drops from the roots, wrap the root mass with burlap. Palms with crownshafts, including *Roystonea*, have sensitive growth buds. To protect the bud, splint the crown with 2x4 lumber tied around each trunk. The splint should extend past the top fronds. Don't underestimate the weight. Depending on the size, you may need to hire a tree service to relocate the palm.

Planting depth. Like palms grown in containers, plant your palm at the same depth that it was previously growing. Never mound soil around the palm's smooth trunk area. Planting a palm too deeply, even by a few inches, can cause decline and death. Similarly, palms planted in a shallow hole will lack the stability they need to grow. New, emerging roots will not reach the soil. To remedy, mound up the soil around the roots.

Soil. In general, transplanted palms should be planted in well-draining soil. Some professsional tree companies recommend backfilling the hole around the rootball with pure cinders, claiming the newly severed roots are susceptible to disease and decay if exposed to contaminated organic material.

After care. Regular watering is the most critical element to ensure your success. Begin fertilizing after four months when roots begin to grow. New root growth is often accompanied by new leaf growth. Expect your palm to produce new fronds within six to 12 months.

Adding to Your Collection

PROPAGATING FROM SEED IS AN INEXPENSIVE AND REWARDING WAY TO GROW MORE PALMS

Growing palms from seed is relatively easy, but some species take months to germinate, or sprout. Many palm seeds are covered with a protective coating that inhibits growth, allowing the seed to lie dormant until ideal weather conditions arrive. Nature eventually breaks down the seed coating to allow germination. Many commercial growers replicate this process with sulfuric acid, but most palm seeds will germinate with the techniques shown here.

Before you begin, pick fresh ripe seed that is not old or decayed. The ripe flesh is typically yellow, orange, or red, but palm fruit can be white, black, brown, or blue. Green fruit is harder to germinate. The easiest way to sprout palm seeds is the "plastic bag" method, which requires only a few common household items.

GROWING PALMS FROM SEED

You'll need a few basic items to grow palms from seed: plastic gloves; large, zip-type plastic storage bags; sterile spaghnum peat moss or coir; and a sharp knife.

❶ **Soak the palm fruit** in water for 24-72 hours, changing the water daily. Soaking ferments the fruit and makes it easy to remove the fleshy pulp. Wear gloves; many palm fruits contain stinging crystals of calcium oxalate that will irritate your skin.

❷ **Drain the water and remove the fleshy fruit.** Use a sharp knife to peel away the flesh from the seed. To clean a large quantity, use a window screen or rock tumbler with gravel and water. Wash away all remaining pulp to prevent mold.

❸ **Soak the cleaned seeds** in warm water for another 24-72 hours. Viable seeds will sink. Remove and discard any floating seeds.

❹ **Soak the planting medium** in water to make sure it is completely saturated. Then squeeze the planting medium with your fist to remove excess water. The planting media should be moist, not wet. If the planting media is too wet, it will likely grow mold. To prevent fungus, mist the seeds with fungicide available at most garden centers.

❺ **Place damp planting media and palm seeds in a plastic bag** and seal tight. Then place the bag in a warm, dark location. If possible, place the bag in an area where it can receive bottom heat, such as on a water heating tank or electric heating mat. Seeds germinate quickly at about 80°F/30°C.

❻ **Check for progress every few days.** If the planting medium is soggy, leave the bag open for a few hours. If it is too dry, mist with a mixture of water and fungicide. Seeds may begin to sprout in as little as a week, though some seeds may take more than a year.

❼ **Plant in tall narrow containers.** If the seed is still attached, don't remove it. The seedling will receive nourishment from the seed for months. Use well-draining soil kept moist, but not wet. Place your seedlings in bright, indirect light. Repot when the roots have filled the container.

Making Palms Look Great

WITH A LITTLE MAINTENANCE, YOUR PALMS WILL LOOK FANTASTIC ALL YEAR LONG

Like all plants, palms have specific cultural requirements for food and water. The best way to know if you are providing the right care for your palm trees is simple: look at them. Examine the leaves closely. They should be green and devoid of any stripes and speckles. Look closely for insects. While palms are not particularly susceptible to pests, spider mites and scale may be present. Examine the trunk for signs of distress or decay. Cracks may be signs of overwatering; a pinched trunk is usually the sign of drought stress.

Watering. Basic maintenance requires a good watering routine. Palms prefer long, thorough soaks over short, frequent sprays. Palms planted in turfgrass may not receive a deep enough soak to encourage a strong root system. The amount of water you give your palm depends on a number of factors, including:

- **Age.** Young trees require frequent waterings.
- **Temperature.** Higher temperatures mean frequent watering.
- **Humidity.** Increase watering frequency in dry air climates.
- **Wind.** Wind desiccates palm fronds. Frequent watering reduces stress.
- **Shade.** Plants in shade typically require less frequent watering.
- **Rainfall.** Palms in high rainfall areas require less irrigation.

In Hawai'i's low rainfall areas, most growers recommend installing a drip irrigation system to water palms. A drip system provides a targeted trickle of water to the palm's root system. These systems are inexpensive and easy to install. The best alternative is a weekly soak with a garden hose.

A good way to know if your palm is getting enough water is to dig a small, deep hole about 2 ft./.5 m. away from the palm's trunk. Check to see if the water is penetrating the surface and reaching the root zone.

Mulching. Mulch not only looks nice, it retains moisture, regulates the soil temperature, and reduces the spread of weeds, which can rob water and harbor insects. Remove turfgrass and any plants that are growing within two feet of your palm's trunk, then spread a two-inch layer of decomposed, organic material around the trunk. Be careful not to bank the mulch up against the trunk; leave a six-inch gap between the palm's trunk and the ring of mulch.

Weeding. Weeds harbor insects and steal water and nutrients from the palm. Hand weed around your palms or lay weed fabric around the tree. Cover the weed fabric with mulch. Don't use plastic sheets or tarps. Plastic does not breathe and will reduce the flow of air and water to the roots. If you have a large number of weeds to remove, spray an herbicide around the trunk. Do not use herbicides around young palms or new stems of mature clumping species.

Fertilizing. Palms are heavy feeders with unique fertilizer needs. The most common problems are potassium and magnesium deficiencies. In older leaves, potassium deficiency can be identified by leaves which appear translucent yellow with speckles or spots of dead tissue. Use potassium sulfate to prevent this problem in new leaves. Commonly called "curly top," magnesium deficiency can be identified by leaves which have broad bands of yellow on the outer margins of the leaves. Common Epsom salts can be sprinkled around the root zone to increase the magnesium in the soil.

The best palm fertilizers have a ratio of the following nutrients:

- 3 parts nitrogen (N)
- 1 part phosphorus (P)
- 3 parts potassium (K)

18N-6P-18K is a common formula with this ratio. Make sure your fertilizer also includes a complete minor element package, essential in Hawai'i's poor soils. Some of the best commercial fertilizers are called controlled-release formulas. These fertilizers are encapsulated and continue to fertilize the palm over a period of several months. Some are released by moisture and some by temperature. Depending on rain or temperature in an area, the fertilizer may not last as many months as the manufacturer states. Organic fertilizers require more frequent application but have the added benefit of improving the soil. Cottonseed meal is a good basis for an organic routine. Supplement with additional nutrients to fit your specific needs. With all fertilizers, make sure you read the manufacturer's instructions. Most fertilizers are composed of salts which will toxify the soil to some extent. Overuse may damage the plant.

Fertilize the roots, not the trunk. Broadcast your fertilizer in a wide band around your palm up to 15 feet for large, mature palms. Most palm fertilizers specify you spread 1.5 pounds of palm fertilizer per 100 square feet in the growing zone. Neighboring plants will benefit from the additional fertilizer they receive.

Pruning. Pruning is sometimes a matter of aesthetics. You may prefer to remove the dead fronds from your tree or leave them alone for a more natural appearance. But, beware: Rodents and insects nest in the dead fronds of palms. In general, only remove brown fronds from your palm trees. Palms translocate nutrients from dying green fronds to new growth. If you remove the green fronds, you will deprive the palm of vital nutrients and slow its growth. Memorize this rule: If it's brown, cut it down. Bypass pruners are ideal for trimming dead fronds, but scissors can be used to remove brown leaf tips on smaller palms. For taller trees, purchase a telescopic pruner or hire a tree maintenance service.

Palms with crownshafts, like royal palms (*Roystonea* species) are considered self-pruning. As fronds die, they fall to the ground, leaving a clean leaf scar on the trunk. Others, like the Mexican fan palm (*Washingtonia robusta*) retain dead fronds and form a "petticoat" of brown leaves that must be removed by hand.

PRUNING RULES

To promote growth and vitality in your palms, follow these basic rules:

❶ **Only remove brown fronds.** Palms reabsorb nutrients from fading fronds. Only remove dead or diseased fronds from your palm. Most people make the mistake of trimming away viable fronds from a palm's canopy. As their fronds begin to yellow and die, palms translocate nutrients to other parts of the plant. Cutting these fronds before they have turned brown will rob the tree of valuable nutrients and slow the palm's growth.

❷ **Prune during the dry season.** Wounds in the wet season promote fungal growth.

❸ **Use sharp pruning shears.** Carefully cut the fronds close to the trunk. Some trees, such as those in the *Phoenix* genus, may require a large pruning saw or professional care.

❹ **Disinfect pruning equipment** between trees with a 10-minute soak in a 5 percent bleach solution. Dirty equipment spreads lethal diseases.

❺ **Never remove fronds that are held above a horizontal plane.** Some tree trimmers make the mistake of cutting too many fronds, giving the palm a "feather duster" look. Only remove fronds that hang down. Don't remove fronds that are close to the growth spear.

Telescopic pruners make trimming fronds on tall trees easy. Most pruners extend your reach by 20 ft./6 m. and include a saw blade and a bypass pruner. Make sure you purchase a pruner with a rigid saw blade. Inexpensive, flimsy blades make pruning significantly more difficult.

Pests and Diseases

THE MOST COMMON PROBLEMS AFFECTING PALMS

Palm trees are not very susceptible to pests and diseases. Most can be controlled with treatments purchased at a local garden or home improvement center. In extreme cases, plants must be removed and disposed of to prevent the spread of infection.

Insects. Most insect infestations are controlled by predators, including beneficial insects and small animals and birds. The most common insects, particularly on indoor container palms, include spider mites, aphids, and scale. Aphids and scale can be controlled with soapy water. Spray the entire palm, including the undersides of fronds. Treat severe infestations with systemic pesticides that can be applied as a drench or granular application at the root zone. Within a few weeks, your palm will translocate the pesticide through its system and make the palm virtually immune to most insects. Prevention is the best defense against insects. Make sure your palms are well watered, fertilized, and located in a weed-free area. Remove brown, dead fronds that harbor colonies of insects.

Fusarium wilt. Fusarium wilt is a problem in some palms, including date palms (*Phoenix* species). Leaves decline and wilt, leaving just a few fronds standing erect. The disease is spread by infested seeds, soil, and pruning equipment, particularly chain saws. No cure exists; palms must be destroyed. To prevent spreading, sterilize pruning equipment with a 10-minute soak in a 5 percent bleach solution.

Lethal yellowing. Lethal yellowing is a major problem throughout the world, although not common in Hawai'i. The disease attacks many palms, including coconut palms (*Cocos nucifera*) and Christmas palms (*Adonidia merrillii*). Spread by a small leafhopper, this disease causes yellowing of the fronds. Eventually, the palm will collapse. Very little can be done to cure this disease.

Ganoderma butt rot. This disease is fatal and usually attacks older palms. It usually starts in a trunk wound and then attacks the entire tree. This fungal disease looks like a large conch shell at the base of the trunk. Remove affected trees and fumigate the surrounding soil.

Phytophthera. This fatal pathogen rots the roots and crowns of palms. The fungus is spread by birds, insects, and unsanitary pruning equipment. If caught early, arborists can inject the palm with potassium phosphate to boost the immune system. Usually by the time the rot is apparent, it is too late to save the palm.

PREVENTING INFECTION

Here are three easy ways to help prevent soilborne diseases:

❶ **Make sure your palm's soil is well-drained.** Replace the soil in container palms every two years with fresh soil that allows air to penetrate the roots.

❷ **Don't overwater container specimens.** Palm roots require air as well as water to grow. Never let a container palm sit in water, unless it is one of the few aquatic species.

❸ **Use clean pruning equipment.** Make sure pruning equipment is sterilized with bleach or alcohol after trimming each palm.

Exploring Hawai'i's Botanical Gardens

HAWAI'I'S BOTANICAL GARDENS PROVIDE INSPIRATION TO CREATE YOUR OWN TROPICAL RETREAT

O'AHU

Foster Botanical Garden
50 North Vineyard Boulevard
Honolulu, HI 96817
(808) 522-7065
www.honolulu.gov/parks/hbg/fbg.htm

Planted in the 1850s, Foster Botanical Garden is the oldest of the Honolulu Botanical Gardens. This 14-acre garden has an excellent collection of *Pritchardia* palms and rarities like the double coconut (*Lodoicea maldivica*). Open daily from 9 a.m. to 4 p.m. except holidays. Admission fee.

Ho'omaluhia Botanical Garden
45-680 Luluku Road
Kāne'ohe, HI 96744
(808) 233-7323
www.honolulu.gov/parks/hbg/hmbg.htm

Ho'omaluhia displays plantings from the major tropical regions around the world with a special emphasis on native Hawaiian plants. More than 400 acres of gardens with a jaw-dropping view of the Ko'olau Mountains. Open daily from 9 a.m. to 4 p.m. except some holidays. No entrance fee. Guided nature hikes are offered.

Koko Crater Botanical Garden
Inside Koko Crater
(808) 522-7060
www.honolulu.gov/parks/hbg/kcbg.htm

This 60-acre garden is located inside Koko Crater on the eastern side of the island and displays a good selection of palms for dry gardens. No admission fee.

Lyon Arboretum
3860 Manoa Road
Honolulu, HI 96822
(808) 988-0456
wwwdev.hawaii.edu/lyonarboretum/

At the upper end of Mānoa Road, this 194-acre garden features an extensive collection of palms in a rain forest setting. Open daily from 9 a.m. to 4 p.m. except holidays. Guided tours offered

Ho'omaluhia Botanical Garden in Kāne'ohe on O'ahu is a great place to view palms.

on some days. Call (808) 988-0456 for reservations. Admission fee.

Wahiawa Botanical Garden

1396 California Avenue
Wahiawā, HI 96786
(808) 621-7321
www.honolulu.gov/parks/hbg/wbg.htm

Developed by sugar planters in the 1920s and now 27 acres of tropical rain forest gardens. A small collection of palms. Open daily from 9:00 a.m. to 4:00 p.m. except some holidays. No admission fee.

Waimea Valley Audubon Center

59-864 Kamehameha Highway
Hale'iwa, HI, 96712
(808) 638-9199
www.audubon.org/local/sanctuary/Brochures/Waimea.html

Across from Waimea Beach Park on the North Shore. Plant collections include native Hawaiian plants, Polynesian introductions and a palm garden. Open daily 9:30 a.m. to 5 p.m. except some holidays. Admission varies.

BIG ISLAND

Hawaii Tropical Botanical Garden

27-717 Old Mamalahoa Highway
Papaikou, HI 96781
(808) 964-5233
www.htbg.com

Located eight miles north of Hilo on the four-mile Scenic Route, this garden cascades down a slope to Onomea Bay. Stands of Alexandra palms have naturalized on the hillsides. Open seven days a week from 9 a.m. to 5 p.m. Last admission is at 4 p.m. Tours are self-guided and maps are provided. Admission fee.

Nani Mau Gardens

421 Makalika Street
Hilo, HI 96720
(808) 959-3500
www.nanimau.com

South of Hilo off of Highway 11, this 20-acre garden showcases a variety of palms and tropicals. Open daily from 9 a.m. to 4:30 p.m. Admission fee.

Pana'ewa Rainforest Zoo

Hilo, HI
(808) 959-9233
www.hilozoo.com

Large collection of palms in a beautiful setting. A "palm map" is available for free at the gift shop. Open daily from 9 a.m. to 4 p.m. No admission fee.

World Botanical Gardens and Umauma Falls

16 Mile Marker, Highway 19
Umauma, HI
(808) 963-5427
www.wbgi.com

North of Hilo, this garden displays more than 5,000 plant species and Umauma Falls, a three-tiered 300 foot waterfall. Open daily from 9 a.m. to 5:30 p.m. Admission fee.

KAUA'I

National Tropical Botanical Garden

3530 Papalina Road

Kalāheo, HI 96741
(808) 332-7324
http://ntbg.org

Allerton Garden and McBryde Garden are located on the south side of Kaua'i. Queen Emma, wife of King Kamehameha IV, planted a variety of tropical plants, some of which survive in the garden. Allerton and McBryde gardens maintain a wide variety of palms. Open daily. Call for hours and admission fees.

Limahuli Garden is set in a tropical valley on the North Shore. Selected by the American Horticultural Society as the best natural botanical garden in the United States, Limahuli Garden displays ancient taro terraces built nearly a century ago. Features an extensive collection of native plants, including loulu (*Pritchardia*) palms.

MAUI

Kahanu Gardens

Hana, HI
(808) 248-8912
http://ntbg.org/gardens/kahanu.php

Home to Pi'ilanihale Heiau, believed to be the largest ancient place of worship in Polynesia. Features loulu palms (*Pritchardia* species), coconut palms (*Cocos nucifera*), and early Polynesian introductions. Open weekdays from 10 a.m. to 2 p.m. Admission fee.

Palm Organizations

ORGANIZATIONS AROUND THE WORLD TO HELP YOU LEARN MORE ABOUT PALMS

International Palm Society
P.O. Box 7075
Lawrence, KS 66044 USA
www.palms.org

The International Palm Society was founded in 1956 and includes 3,000 members in 81 countries. The society publishes a journal, holds regional events, and hosts a website filled with information about palms.

UNITED STATES

HAWAI'I

Hawai'i Island Palm Society
PO Box 1585, Keaau, HI 96749

The Palm Society of Maui
PO Box 893, Paia, Maui, HI 96779

ARIZONA

International Palm Society, Arizona
13621 North 15th Drive
Phoenix, AZ 85023

CALIFORNIA

Palm Society of Southern California
www.palmssc.org

Northern California Chapter
www.palmsnc.org

FLORIDA

Central Florida Palm & Cycad Society
www.plantapalm.com/centralfl

Florida First Coast Chapter, IPS
[northeastern Florida]
721 Fruitcove Road
Jacksonville, FL 32259
Email: jctimyan@atlantic.com

Palm & Cycad Society of Florida
www.plantapalm.com

Palm Beach Palm and Cycad Society
P.O. Box 3662, Lantana FL 33465-3662

Palm & Cycad Society of Southwest Florida
www.plantapalm.com/southwestfl/

Palm Organizations

South Florida Chapter, IPS
30150 SW 170 Avenue
Homestead, FL 33030
www.plantapalm.com/southfl/

SOUTHEAST USA

**Southeastern Palm and
Exotic Plant Society**
http://sepalms.org

Gulf Coast Chapter, IPS
1957 Antoine Street
Mobile, AL 36606

Louisiana Palm and Cycad Society
114 Melrose Drive
Destrehan, LA 70047
www.LouisianaPalmAndCycadSociety.org

PACIFIC NORTHWEST

**The Pacific Northwest
Palm & Exotic Plant Society**
www.hardypalm.com

TEXAS

Palm Society of South Texas
www.palmsocietysouthtexas.org

Houston, Texas Chapter, IPS
www.palms.org/houston/

WORLDWIDE

AUSTRALIA

Palm & Cycad Societies of Australia
PO Box 1134,
Milton, QLD 4064 Australia
http://pacsoa.org.au/index.html

EL SALVADOR

**Asociacion de Palmera y
Cicas de El Salvador**
Email: rodrigo@bismarckia.com

EUROPE

European Palm Society
34 Keats Avenue
Romford, Essex, RM3 7AR, UK
www.palmsociety.org

FRANCE

Fous de Palmiers
Manatte, F-32460
Le Houga, FR
www.chez.com/palmiers/

NEW CALEDONIA

Association Chambeyronia
PO Box 1132
98 845 Noumea, CEDEX
Email: pierson@socatrans.nc

NEW ZEALAND

Palm Society of New Zealand
PO Box 3871, Auckland, NZ
Email: mscragg_nz@yahoo.com

SOUTH AFRICA

South African Palm Society
PO Box 48309, Hercules, 0030
Republic of South Africa
Phone: +27 12 376 2733
www.sapalm.co.za

SPAIN

**La Asociación Espanola
de Amigos de las Palmas**
c/o Tomás Font Beato Galvez 9-1
Valencia 46007 Spain
Email: deborah@ctv.es

VENEZUELA

Avepalmas
www.avepalmas.org/

JOIN A LOCAL CLUB

To learn more about palms, join one of Hawai'i's local chapters of the International Palm Society:

The International Palm Society supports two local affiliates in Hawaii, one on Maui, the other on the Big Island.

Founded in 1974, the Hawaii Island Palm Society (HIPS) is the largest, with about 200 members dedicated to promoting new and interesting palm species into island landscaping and to providing information about palms and their culture.

Members have planted more than 100 palm species at the Pana'ewa Rainforest Zoo near Hilo to demonstrate the diversity of palms that grow in Hawai'i. HIPS continues to plant and maintain palms at the zoo.

Palm society chapters host educational speakers, garden tours, palm auctions, and BBQs.

To join a local chapter of the International Palm Society or get more information, visit www.palms.org and click on "Affiliated Chapters."

Barrow, Sasha. 1998. A Revision of Phoenix. London. Reprinted from Kew Bulletin 53 (3).

Broschat, Timothy K., and Alan W. Meerow. 2000. Ornamental Palm Horticulture. Gainesville, Florida: University Press of Florida.

Dransfield, John, and Henk Beentje. 1995. The Palms of Madagascar. London: Board of Trustees of the Royal Botanic Gardens: Kew.

Ellison, Don, and Anthony Ellison. 2001. Betrock's Cultivated Palms of the World. Hollywood, Florida: Betrock Information Systems.

Gibbons, Martin. 1993. Palms. Seacaucus, New Jersey: Chartwell Books.

Henderson, Andrew, Gloria Galeano, and Rodrigo Bernal. 1995. Palms of the Americas. Princeton, New Jersey: Princeton University Press.

Hodel, Donald R., ed. 1998. The Palms and Cycads of Thailand. Lawrence, Kansas: Allen Press.

Hodel, Donald R. 1992. Chamaedorea Palms: The Species and their Cultivation. Lawrence, Kansas: Allen Press.

Jones, David L. 1995. Palms Throughout the World. Washington, D.C.: Smithsonian Institution Press.

Leaser, David E. 2007. Betrock's Essential Guide to Palms. Florida: Betrock Information Systems, Inc.

Leaser, David E. 2005. Palms Trees: A Story in Photographs. Los Angeles, California: Westwood Pacific Publishing.

Meerow, Alan W. 1992. Betrock's Guide to Landscape Palms. Cooper City, Florida: Betrock Information Systems, Inc.

Osborn, B., T. Reynoso and G. Stein. 2000. Palms for Southern California – A Quick Reference Guide to Palms. Third Edition. The Palm Society of Southern California.

Principes (later Palms). 1956-2006. Journal of the International Palm Society, Lawrence, Kansas. Vols. 1-50.

Riffle, Robert Lee, and Paul Craft. 2003. An Encyclopedia of Cultivated Palms. Portland, Oregon: Timber Press.

Romney, David H. 1997. Growing Coconuts in South Florida. Homestead, Florida: David H. Romney.

Sunset. 2001. Western Garden Book. Menlo Park, California: Sunset Publishing Corp.

Uhl, Natalie W., and John Dransfield. 1987. Genera Palmarum. Lawrence, Kansas: L.H. Bailey Hortorium and International Palm Society.

Warren, William. 1997. The Tropical Garden. New York: Thames and Hudson, Inc.

Adventitious roots. Roots that form on the trunk of the tree. All palms produce adventitious roots.

Acidic. A pH value below 7. See pH.

Alkaline. A pH value above 7.

Armed. With spines.

Chlorosis. Yellowing of palm fronds due to nutritional deficiencies.

Clumping palm. Palm that forms multiple stems or trunks.

Crownshaft. A smooth, sometimes shiny, area that separates the trunk from the fronds in some palms.

Cultivar. A variety or form that is known only in cultivation.

Frond. The leaf of the palm.

Genus. A group of related species, usually categorized by similarity or origin. The Cuban royal palm is a member of the *Roystonea* genus. Plural is genera.

Glaucous. Blue or blue-gray color on leaves covered with a waxy layer.

Inflorescence. The flower stalk.

Inflorescence bract. A boat-shaped bract that covers the inflorescence.

Leaf base. The wide area of the leaf, or frond, that attaches to the trunk.

Leaf scar. The conspicuous remnant of a fallen frond on the trunk.

Necrotic. Dead or dying plant tissue.

Palmate. Used to describe fan palm leaves.

Petiole. The primary stalk which supports the indivual leaves of the palm.

pH. A measure of the acidity or alkalinity. Usually refers to the soil or water in gardening.

Pinnate. Used to describe feather-shaped palm leaves.

Plumose. Feather-shaped palm leaves that form on various planes, giving the frond a fuller look.

Species. A distinct entity, or type of palm, in a genus. The species name follows the genus. For example, *Roystonea regia* is the correct genus and species for the Cuban royal palm.

Subtropical. Located between the Tropic latitudes and the Temperate latitudes.

Spine. Sharp, rigid, pointed protrusions on various parts of some palms.

Stilt roots. Aerial roots that form at the base of the trunk to support the tree. Palms with stilt roots seem to walk on top of their surrounding soil.

Unarmed. Free of spines.

Trunk. The main stem of the palm.

Variegated. Marked with streaks of different colors.

Acknowledgements

When you dive into the world of palms, you not only expand your knowledge of these amazing plants, you also meet some of the nicest people.

I'd particularly like to thank Claudia Cannon from the Islander Group. Sitting in her Mililani office, Claudia outlined the book you are now holding. Mutual Publishing's staff, including Jane Gillespie and Angela Britten, made the book a reality.

Members of the International Palm Society, botanical institutions and palm growers provided accurate, up-to-date information on the culture and care of palms. Subject matter was reviewed by key members of the International Palm Society, including Scott Zona, Don Hodel, Randy Moore, and Billy Olson. Karen Piercy, Bo Lundkvist, and Jenny Johnson from the Hawaii Island Palm Society helped tailor the cultural information to ensure its accuracy.

I visited all of the major botanical gardens throughout the Islands and was greeted warmly by their staffs. Jonel Smith and Winnie Singeo exemplify the graciousness of the Honolulu Botanical Gardens. On the mainland, Jim Folsom, Dani Rudeen, and Melanie Thorpe from the Huntington Library, Art Collections, & Botanical Gardens, supported my previous book on palms and inspired me to write another.

To fill out my portfolio of photos, I traveled to Florida to visit two of the world's premier palm gardens, the Fairchild Tropical Botanic Garden and the Montgomery Botanical Center. Thank you, Mike Maunder and the staff of the Fairchild for your help.

The Montgomery Botanical Center, a nonprofit institution devoted to advancing the science of tropical botany, displays an impressive collection of rare and exotic palms. Thanks to Patrick Griffith, Larry Noblick, Laurie Danielson, and the staff at MBC, I was invited to photograph the collection for my work on this book.

Thanks also to the nurserymen, growers, and landscapers who provided real-world care information. Chris Oppenheimer from Botanics Wholesale invited me to his extensive South Florida growing grounds to see how large-scale commercial growers care for palms. Robert Davie, a leading landscape architect, provided insight to landscaping with palms. And landscaper Domingo Gonzalez helped with pruning techniques.

Finally, thanks to my family and friends for their help, including Terrance Leaser, Tammy and Richard Guerra, Emi Harnden, Bob Redpath, Matt Ingebrigtsen, Heidi Wulkow, and Joseph and Elizabeth Leaser.

Index

Index

David Leaser has authored several books and journal articles about palms. His book, *Palm Trees: A Story in Photographs*, is the first coffee-table book ever written on palms. Endorsed by the International Palm Society, the book has received critical acclaim from horticultural societies and leading authorities on palm trees around the world, including the Royal Botanical Garden at Kew.

Leaser also authored *Betrock's Essential Guide to Palms*, a comprehensive guide to palm care for gardeners, landscapers, and homeowners.

A long-time member of the International Palm Society and the International Plant Propagators Society, Leaser is in demand as a featured speaker at botanical gardens and garden centers throughout the United States, including the Los Angeles Arboretum, the San Francisco Botanical Garden, the Huntington Library, Art Collections, and Botanical Gardens, and the San Diego Zoo. He lectures on a variety of topics, including "Good Palms for Small Gardens," "Landscaping with Palms," and "Seven Surprising Uses for Palms."

Leaser has also written articles for publications, including *Garden Compass Magazine* and the *Palm Journal*, and his photos have appeared in *Sunset Magazine, Islands Magazine,* and various palm-related journals and newspapers. He is frequently interviewed on palm-oriented topics by radio programs and publications, including Garden Compass Radio, Garden Talk Radio, the *Los Angeles Times,* the *Los Angeles Daily Breeze,* the *Malibu Surfside News* and the *Sunset Western Garden Book.*

A graduate of Pepperdine University, Leaser received the Pacemaker® award for excellence in journalism. He received his master's degree from the University of Southern California and also attended the University of Hawai'i at Manoa. Mr. Leaser recently sold his farm on the Big Island of Hawai'i and presently resides in Los Angeles, California.